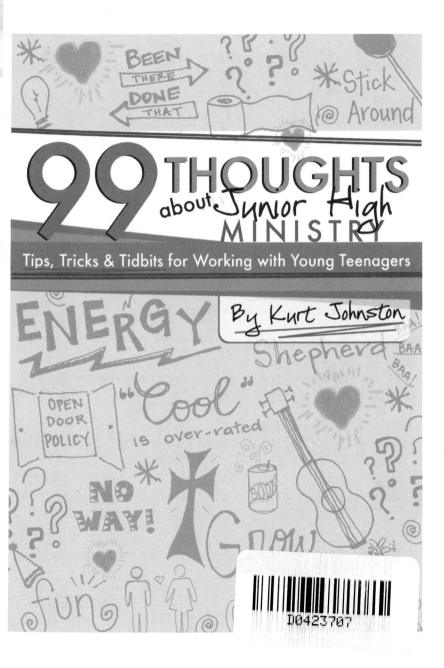

99 Thoughts About Junior High Ministry:
Tips, Tricks, and Tidbits for Working With Young Teenagers

Copyright © 2012 Kurt Johnston

group.com
simplyyouthministry.com

Credits
Author: Kurt Johnston
Executive Developer: Nadim Najm
Chief Creative Officer: Joani Schultz
Editor: Rob Cunningham
Art Director: Veronica Preston
Production Manager: DeAnne Lear

ISBN 978-0-7644-8258-8

10 9 8 7 6 5 4 3 2   20 19 18 17 16 15 14 13 12

Printed in the United States of America.

CONTENTS

INTRODUCTION

You may be thinking, *"This book is so tiny, it will fit in my pocket!"* Congratulations! You are very gifted at the art of book assessment at a glance. And the reason I wrote this tiny, pocket-sized book is so that you may also become very gifted in the art of junior high ministry.

This book contains exactly 99 thoughts, tips, tricks, and tidbits that I hope will encourage you, equip you, and excite you on your junior high ministry journey—whether you are a seasoned, full-time veteran or a brand-new volunteer.

There are two ways you can utilize this book: First, you can read it in about 20 minutes, nod your head in agreement or disagreement a few times, then use it as a coaster at home. I suppose that's OK—everybody needs coasters. Or you can read it in about 20 minutes, highlight the 10-15 thoughts that pop out from the rest, and prayerfully consider how those thoughts might be implemented in your junior high ministry context.

I hope you'll go for Option 2—partly because my fragile ego can't handle the idea of a book I wrote, no matter how tiny, being used as a coaster, but mostly because I know that if you prayerfully put a few of these thoughts into practice, your junior high ministry will be better for it!

Partnering with you,

Kurt Johnston

PROGRAMMING, TEACHING, AND CREATIVITY

1 REMEMBER: Caring adult + JHer = Good stuff!

This book is chock-full of thoughts, tidbits, and transformational ideas! But if you try to implement everything on these pages, you'll drive yourself crazy. It's junior high ministry; don't overthink it! The reality is that as long as you are connecting junior highers to caring adults who love Jesus, good ministry will be the result. The rest is icing on the cake.

2 THE DEFINITION OF PROGRAMS:
The stuff your ministry does.

In recent years, programs have gotten a bad rap. Uttering the word *program* in some junior high ministry circles has become taboo. Let me redefine the word. Programs = The Stuff Your Ministry Does. That's it! Every ministry does stuff, and the stuff you do can accurately be defined as programs. If you don't want to use the word *programs* to refer to your camps, fun outings, Bible studies, strategically informal gatherings, and the like, I suppose that's fine—even though that's what they are.

3 LEVERAGE THE POWER of the "one-two punch."

Over the years, I've discovered that God often uses a one-two punch to grab a hold of the hearts of junior highers. The one-two punch is the powerful combination of a relationship with a caring adult (see Thought 1) and spiritual markers. Spiritual markers are those special moments at camp, on a retreat, during a mission trip, or in a seemingly normal midweek program when the Holy Spirit does something memorable in the heart of a young student. As you organize your ministry to young teenagers, think about the power of the one-two punch and how you can best create an atmosphere for it to happen.

4 INSTEAD OF WORKING to keep students' attention, work to keep their interest; if they're interested, they will pay attention.

I have a confession: I'm not interested in knitting. And because I'm not interested in knitting, if an old lady tried to lecture me for 20 minutes on "The Joys of Knitting," I would have a hard time faking like I cared. The same thing is true in your junior high ministry—specifically, when it comes to your lesson time. Junior highers will give their attention to stuff that interests them.

Work to make your lessons interesting, and you'll be shocked at how well students actually pay attention!

5 YOUR LESSON DOESN'T NEED TO BE LONG
to be good—but if it's going to be long, it had BETTER be good!

I'm convinced that the only people who like long sermons are preachers. Longer isn't better—better is better! When you are prepping a lesson, ask yourself, "What is the best way to help junior highers grasp this truth in around 20 minutes?"

6 INSTEAD OF SETTING ONE BAR for all of your students to reach, set lots of bars and challenge students as individuals.

It's tempting to set one goal—one bar you hope every student will grab for—and program toward that end. There's nothing wrong with saying things like, "This year, we want everybody to invite a friend" or "Our goal this summer is that every one of you would go on a mission trip." But by doing so, you set one bar for everybody in your group, and it's a bar that may be too high for some and not high enough for others.

Because every junior higher in your ministry is at a different place developmentally and spiritually, I think it's more beneficial to look for ways to get to know each student God has placed under your care and to see how you might be able to set a "bar" that is unique to each of them.

7 WHEN TEACHING, put yourself in your students' shoes; don't always expect them to put themselves in yours.

Your junior highers haven't gone to college yet, so limit your college analogies. They aren't married, so use stories about your marriage sparingly. They aren't as interested in Mosaic law and how it affects a New Testament view of grace as you are, so avoid the temptation to write small group curriculum on the subject. When you teach, don't expect them to enter your adult world; instead, it is your job to enter their world—their world of insecurities, strained friendships, problems with mom and dad, and wondering if there is such a thing as too much Axe® body spray.

8 GET INPUT from your JHers, and then use your filter.

Junior highers know what they like and what they don't. They are fun, funny, and creative. They have lots of opinions about your ministry that are worth listening to. What they don't have is a ton of experience, discernment, or common sense. Regularly gather ideas and input from them, and then use your "adult filter" to figure out which ideas are awesome and which ideas are awesome but will result in bodily harm!

9 BUILD "strategic interruptions" into your lessons.

I learned this one from my friend Mark Oestreicher. The reality is this: If you don't build a few interruptions into your lesson, your junior highers will do the job for you! You've been there: a loud burp, a tossed paper airplane, an eighth-grade girl suddenly falling out of her chair. And it always seems to happen at the most important part of your lesson! Look for ways to intentionally build interruptions into your lesson that give students opportunities to laugh, mingle, and move around. This way, you can use their energy to your advantage.

10 BEING CREATIVE IS EASY!

Guess what? You are creative. You may not feel creative, but you are. Here's how I know: You were once 5 years old, and every 5-year-old is creative!

You didn't outgrow your ability to be creative; you just quit practicing. As we get older, we are told to color inside the lines, to quit talking to our imaginary friends, to stop daydreaming, and other brilliant instructions. Junior high ministry is a GREAT place to reclaim your creative side. First, redefine what it means to be creative. I'll give you a simple definition: Creativity is simply the willingness to try something new. Second, look for easy places to try new stuff, and take a swing! If you swing and miss, it's no big deal; junior highers are a forgiving bunch. They will appreciate the effort.

11 CREATE EXPERIENCES that help JHers discover their gifts.

Don't give your junior highers spiritual gift tests. Instead, provide a variety of opportunities within your ministry to help students experiment and begin to discover how God has wired them. Let them try out for the band. If they don't like it or aren't musically inclined, let them try out for the drama team. If they are terrible actors, let them try out to be a greeter. If they can't say hello to a visitor, let them stack chairs. Everybody can stack chairs!

12 PROVIDE LOTS OF OPPORTUNITIES
for JHers to develop leadership skills.

The junior high years are a perfect time to help young teenagers begin to develop leadership skills. Few are ready to carry significant leadership responsibilities, but don't let that fact keep you from providing opportunities for future leaders to begin to emerge. Instead of creating a full-blown leadership program that only a few students have time for, I suggest you develop the habit of making sure that virtually everything you do gives junior highers a chance to step up and lead. As the "cream rises to the top," skim it off and give those students more and more opportunities!

13 TEACH AND TALK about the tough stuff.

Why do bad things happen to good people? How do I know what is really true and what isn't? What about my friends from a different religion? Can anybody help me figure out this whole sexuality thing?

Don't avoid the tough topics. In fact, make addressing tough topics part of your ministry culture. Your junior highers are asking, wondering, and trying to figure this stuff out. What better atmosphere for them to wrestle through some of life's complexities than in your youth group!

14 **"FUN"** is the universal language of JHers.

Question: If church isn't fun, why in the world would 13-year-olds want to be there?

Answer: They wouldn't.

You don't have to water things down. You don't have to candy-coat the gospel. You don't have to try to entertain kids. But you don't have to bore them to death, either! You don't have to be funny, but you do need to look for ways to create a fun environment that junior high kids will look forward to. And believe it or not, wacky games and young, cool leaders aren't the only sources of fun:

- When you remember a junior higher's name, it helps make church fun.

- When you provide opportunities for discussion, it helps make church fun.

- When you make the learning experiential in nature, it helps make church fun.

- When you follow up on a prayer request from last week, it helps make church fun.

- And yes—when you play a game that involves pudding, it helps make church fun.

15 REMEMBER: EVERYTHING
teaches something.

My friend Scott Rubin likes to refer to this principle as "the hidden curriculum." It's the reality that *everything* that happens in your ministry is teaching *something*, whether you realize it or not. The way new students are treated teaches something. The way grace is shown to troublemakers teaches something. The way the youth pastor treats his or her family teaches something. Every aspect of your junior high ministry is teaching something—all the time. But hey, no pressure!

16 A SPOONFUL OF SUGAR helps the medicine go down.

In addition to being a fun line in a classic show tune, this is a gem of wisdom for those of us working with junior highers. For some students, the idea of sitting through a Bible study or Sunday school class is the equivalent of taking their medicine: They know it's good for them, but it's not very enjoyable! You can change that! Add a little "sugar" to the medicine by telling fun stories, inviting their input, actually smiling while you're teaching, and making other helpful additions.

17 IT'S ALL ABOUT FRIENDS, friends, friends, friends, and friends in JH!

And that's OK! Go with it. Don't spend all your time trying to break up cliques. Don't stay up at night trying to figure out how to get the skaters to hang out with the chess club kids. Instead of being frustrated by the "friendship factor," embrace it. In fact, don't just embrace it; leverage it! Look for ways to help your junior highers develop their friendship skills, strengthen their existing friendships, and be open to new, emerging ones.

18 DON'T KEEP YOUR JHERS SEGREGATED;
look for ways to integrate them with the rest of the church body.

Your junior highers need their own space; they need programs and church experiences designed specifically for them. But they don't need to be separated all the time! In fact, you are doing more harm than good in the long haul if you segregate them completely. Look for opportunities for your junior high group to rub shoulders with the congregation at-large. Volunteer to have your students serve at the senior adult potluck, ask ministries in your church to consider allowing junior highers to serve alongside adults, and look for natural times in the year to cancel junior high Sunday school completely so they are "forced" to sit in big church with mom and dad.

19 QUESTION: WHAT ARE ADULTS DOING
in your JH ministry that you can let JHers do instead?

I asked myself this question not long ago, and the answer was embarrassing: "Way too much!" We have made the hard decision to let students lead music, run the tech room, and serve as greeters.

The music is often really bad, the tech is usually very un-techy, and our visitors get greeted in hideously awkward ways at times! But the trade-off is worth it. Here's something to think about: If a junior higher walks into your setting and sees that it is totally run by adults, what does it feel like? School! And very few junior highers want to go to school another day each week.

20 MIX IT UP!

Keep 'em guessing. Mix up the order of your service on a regular basis. Avoid the temptation to play students' favorite games over and over again. Leave them wanting more. There's no such thing as a good rut.

21 CREATE "NO WAY!" moments.

Once a month or so, we try to create something in our ministry that causes our junior highers to say, "NO WAY!" We go overboard with a set design, play a totally over-the-top game, or mix things up so radically that students think to themselves, "Wow, I can't believe they did that at church this week." Creating "NO WAY!" moments is a fun strategy to get students talking about church long after the service is over.

22 **KEEP A FILE** on each event so you have a record of what worked and what didn't.

This is Junior High Ministry 101 stuff. After any significant event, create a file that you can quickly use as a reference should you ever decide to do that particular activity again. I suggest creating a one-page form that you use for every event. As you plan the event, fill out the form with contacts, price quotes, pros and cons of the event, things to remember next time, and all kinds of other helpful info and details. The next time you decide to do the same activity, half of your work is already done for you because you kept good records.

23 **WHEN PLANNING AN EVENT,** don't reach for the file. Start with a blank slate!

You want a file on each event, but avoid the temptation to start this year's event by grabbing last year's file! Instead, start with a blank slate and dream a little bit. Think creatively about what the perfect version of this event might look like. THEN grab last year's file and see how it can help you.

24 **REMEMBER,** lots of you are smarter than one of you.

I'm not a fan of committees, but I'm not a fan of making decisions in a vacuum, either. Consider creating a little team of adult leaders and students that you can rely on for input, guidance, and creative ideas. Run big decisions past a few folks before moving forward. You are smart but not as smart as you PLUS a handful of others!

25 **LOOK FOR OPPORTUNITIES** for your JHers to minister to the older generation of your church.

Let's face it: Most old people are scared of junior highers. They used to be junior highers, but that was a long time ago. This, combined with the fact that most junior highers are afraid of old people, makes it highly unlikely that the two age groups interact very often. But they need each other! The older saints in your church have SO MUCH to offer young teenagers, and believe it or not, young teenagers have a ton to offer the dusty old people. Here's an easy idea to get you started: Have your junior high group host a dinner-and-movie night for the senior adults. I'm not talking about pizza and Austin Powers, but something more like gourmet chicken and *Gone With the Wind*.

26 CREATING A CALENDAR IS A HASSLE—
but not creating one is a BIGGER hassle!

A little work ahead of time goes a LONG, LONG way. Parents of junior highers like to know what's coming up and how much it's gonna cost. A quarterly calendar that they can stick to the refrigerator sounds old school, but some things never go out of style. Try it. They'll like it!

27 YOU DON'T HAVE TO BE separate
to succeed!

It would be great if you had enough teenagers, volunteers, space, and budget to have separate junior high and high school ministries. But you don't have to be separate to be effective! There are lots of benefits to a youth group that is combined. Here are a few simple ideas to make the most of a combined group:

- Identify leaders who lean more toward junior high, and let them focus on that age group.

- Ask older high school students to mentor a junior higher in the group.

- Look for opportunities throughout the year to provide separate activities for each age group so they get some stuff designed specifically for them.

28 JHERS HAVE ENERGY, and LOTS of it— use it to your advantage.

Walk into the high school meeting area 10 minutes before the service starts. Now, walk into the junior high meeting area. Notice a difference? For most people, when they think of junior highers, they think of energy—and LOTS of it! This isn't good or bad; it just is. And because it just "is," you would be better off figuring out ways to use it to your advantage instead of trying to make junior highers act more like high schoolers. They can't, and you shouldn't want them to!

29 SMALL GROUPS are a BIG deal!

The junior high ministry I lead has two primary programs: a weekly large group gathering that is a "come one, come all" high-energy church experience, and weekly small groups that consist of 8 to 10, same-grade/same-gender junior highers and a couple of adult volunteers. What if I could only do one program; which would I choose?

Without a doubt, I would opt for small groups. Here are just a few reasons small groups are a BIG deal:

- In small groups, students have a better chance of truly being known.

- In small groups, students can ask questions and express doubts.

- In small groups, students can pray for each other and bear each other's burdens.

- In small groups, students learn how to build intimate friendships.

- In small groups, adult volunteers move from chaperones to shepherds.

You may not be able to (or want to) have a completely separate program dedicated to small groups, but you may want to look for ways to provide some level of small group activity. It is well worth the effort.

30 IN SMALL GROUPS, consider separating by grade and gender.

There is certainly more than one way to do small groups, but dividing by grade and gender seems to consistently be the most effective with junior highers. Take another look at some of the benefits of small groups. It seems obvious that many of those benefits are more likely to manifest in a same-grade/same-gender setting. Seventh-grade girls need a place where they can be themselves, and eighth-grade guys do, too.

ADOLESCENT DEVELOPMENT

31 IT'S ALMOST IMPOSSIBLE to exaggerate the power of relationships.

Human beings are wired for relationships. We don't all need them to the same degree, but we all need them. Junior highers are no different. Make it a priority to build into your ministry the value of "helping junior highers develop meaningful relationships." Help them understand the importance of meaningful relationships with their peers, with adults, and with Christ. No junior higher should feel like they are facing the most tumultuous years of life alone!

32 HELP JHERS LEARN the skills to "grow on their own."

One of your biggest responsibilities is to begin to wean junior highers from their dependence on you, the church, and your programs for their spiritual growth. As we all know, church should always play a vital role in the life of a follower of Jesus, but too many people rely on the church as their only means of growing in their faith. Don't handicap your students this way! Instead help them develop spiritual habits such as reading the Bible on their own, serving in ministry, memorizing Scripture, sharing their faith with others, and other healthy habits.

33 IN JH MINISTRY, WE ALWAYS PLANT SEEDS, we always water—and sometimes we even get to harvest!

Why do we so easily forget about this biblical principle? I've got news for you: A whole bunch of the junior highers in your ministry won't truly understand what it means to follow Jesus until they have moved on to high school, college, or adulthood. It isn't your responsibility to make sure every kid who darkens your church door chooses to follow Christ. Your responsibility is to plant seeds, water those seeds, and harvest the ones that God determines are ripe! I remind my team regularly that junior high ministry is a "seed-planting ministry."

34 TO KEEP THINGS AGE-APPROPRIATE, you need to be a student of adolescent development. JHers are different than HSers.

We know this to be true, but many junior high ministries don't reflect our knowledge. Even if your ministry is combined, look for ways to make sure there are aspects of it created to honor the developmental stage of junior highers. Even though adolescence is extending longer and longer, junior highers are still on the very front end of the journey.

If you are unsure of the fundamental stages of development and how junior highers differ from high schoolers, be sure to read up on the subject!

35 DON'T EXPECT JHERS WHO DON'T KNOW JESUS to act like they do.

In fact, don't even expect junior highers who *DO* know Jesus to act like they do! Quit being so frustrated (and feeling like a youth ministry failure) when junior highers behave, well, like junior highers! Remember: You are planting seeds.

36 REMEMBER, IT'S ABOUT WHAT THEY NEED, not what you WANT.

I need to admit something: I'm tired of teaching "Friendship 101" and "How to Be a Good Friend" and "Who Was Moses, and What Does He Have to Do With My Life?" Can't we please move on to something deeper? Actually, NO! Junior high ministry isn't about teaching students the things YOU want as a 20-, 30- or 40-something leader. It is about teaching them what THEY need as 12- to 14-year-olds.

Seventh-grade math teachers would be fired if they decided that, because they were tired of teaching the basics of pre-algebra, they would skip right to calculus. Yet many junior high youth workers do the same thing all too often.

37 WHEN YOU TEACH, make sure every lesson has some "handles."

Don't just give out biblical information; put "handles" on the information! Make sure every lesson has some sort of application attached to it. Handles allow students to carry their learnings with them as they walk through life. As you teach, look for places to include moments of "How to" and "What now?" and "So what?" to ensure you are making the lesson something teenagers can actually apply to their lives.

38 IN A LOT OF WAYS, JH ministry is more like children's ministry than HS ministry. Sorry.

Specifically, when it comes to parents. Like children's ministry, students rely on mom and dad to get them there. Like children's ministry, the level of trust parents have in you will determine the level of participation of their child.

Like children's ministry, moms and dads still ask lots of questions about safety, supervision, and other important details. Instead of working so hard to distance yourself from the children's ministry, I suggest you cozy up to them and learn a few things.

39 EMBRACE THE SQUIGGLE.

If you have read stuff I've written in the past or have heard me teach a junior high ministry workshop, you know that the charge to "embrace the squiggle" is, to me, a key part of enjoying junior high ministry and being effective in your role. To put it quite simply, many people get frustrated working with junior highers because they have a misguided expectation of what spiritual development should look like. See those three pictures? Only one of them is a realistic picture of the spiritual journey your students are on. Can you guess which? My hunch is that it's the one that also most closely resembles your own spiritual journey!

40 PROVIDE LOTS OF OPPORTUNITIES
for questions and discussion.

It's interesting how little room junior highers often are given to ask questions and wrestle with their doubts. School doesn't allow too much of it. (After all, other students who "get it" are in the room, and the teacher needs to power through the lesson plan.) Coaches don't provide much time for it. (Imagine a Pop Warner football player saying, "Hey coach, I have some struggles and doubts with the playbook you've designed.") Parents often shut down questions. ("Don't argue; just do what you're told.") Your ministry can break the mold! Encourage questions, expect students to share their doubts, and permit them to "push back" on something you've taught. Remember the idea of "handles"? Question-asking and discussion time are an easy way to put handles on a lesson.

41 ENCOURAGE JHERS TO EXPRESS
their doubts and to share their struggles.

Don't be intimidated by or frustrated with the fact that junior high students will wonder—and wander. Instead of trying to build in "safety nets" to ensure it won't happen, expect it to happen and create an environment where junior highers feel safe expressing their doubts and struggles instead of feeling like they need to keep them hidden.

42 NORMALIZE, NORMALIZE, NORMALIZE!

Junior highers often convince themselves that they are "the only one":

- "I am the only one who doesn't fit in."

- "I am the only one who doesn't do well at sports."

- "I am the only one who has parents who don't get it."

- "I am the only one who doesn't like the way they look."

When possible, look for ways to normalize the junior high experience. Help junior highers see that their struggles, insecurities, and uncertainties are common.

43 JHERS ARE CAPABLE of so much more than most adults give them credit for!

Austin Gutwein, whose dad is one of my best friends, started a little ministry when he was in fifth grade. It hit its peak when he was in junior high.

During his junior high years, Austin and his ministry, Hoops of Hope, raised well over $1 million for children orphaned by HIV/AIDS.

When I share that our ministry has taken junior highers on mission trips to Kenya, Brazil, the Philippines, Cambodia, and Costa Rica, I almost always get some sort of shocked response. Let's work together to help other adults see the awesome things junior highers are capable of accomplishing!

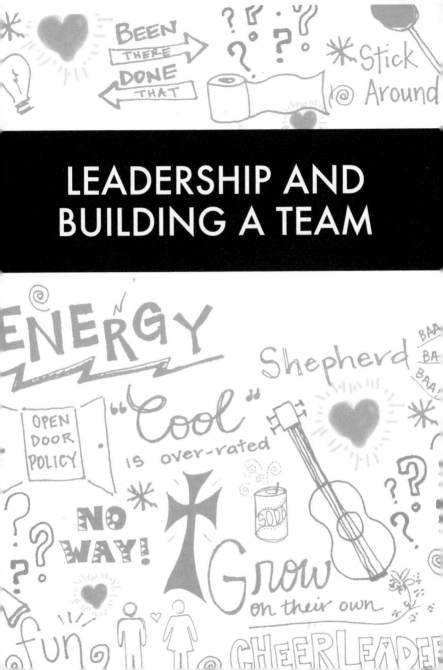

LEADERSHIP AND
BUILDING A TEAM

44 DON'T UNDERESTIMATE the impact older adults can make.

In many churches, there is an untapped pool of potential junior high volunteers: the senior adult Sunday school class! Over the years I have learned over and over again that some of the best junior high leaders are those who have wrinkly skin. John Allen, a 77-year-old with a heart of gold, was one of the best volunteers our ministry has ever seen. He knew most of our students by name, he went to camp as a counselor, and he came to me with more creative ideas than I could put in motion! It was a sad day when he decided it was time to step out of ministry. His reason? He needed to spend more time caring for his aging girlfriend. You heard me right—*girlfriend*!

45 YOU ARE A CHEERLEADER!

One of your most important roles is actually quite simple: You should aim to be one of the biggest cheerleaders in the lives of your students. Cheer them on, share words of encouragement, and stay positive when their chips are down. Sadly, far too many junior highers are surrounded by naysayers. Your job is to be a "hooray-sayer."

46 BE YOURSELF!

When I was in junior high, I asked my mom, "What's the best age to be?"

"Whatever age you currently are," she wisely answered.

A similar principle holds true when it comes to youth work. What's the best kind of youth worker to be? The kind of youth worker you are! Seriously, unless you are using junior highers to smuggle nuclear weapons, you are doing just fine. Don't try to be something or somebody you aren't. Play to your strengths. If you are older, go with it! If you are a deep thinker, great! If you are an introvert, then introvert away! Don't buy into the myth that the best junior high youth workers are young, cool, athletic skaters who know how to play guitar—unless, of course, you happen to be a young, cool, athletic skater who plays guitar!

47 BE SMART about your personal online presence.

Some of your students will want to friend you on Facebook®, follow you on Twitter®, and read your blog. Be wise concerning the content and appropriateness of the things you post. Remember that younger, less mature, and more easily influenced eyes are browsing!

48 BE ON THE LOOKOUT for students who are hurting.

Sadly, many junior highers are hurting, and most of them don't know what to do with their pain. Make it a point to be on the lookout for students in your ministry who need some extra attention and help. You don't need to be an expert in dealing with at-risk teenagers, but you do need to have a plan in place to help give hurting junior highers and their families the support they need.

49 PUT YOUR LEADERS IN A BOX— and then expand the box!

This is one of my favorite leadership practices. Here's the idea: Your leaders need some parameters, but not too many. Figure out what those parameters should be, the box they need to stay within, and then expand the box! In other words, as long as they stay within the parameters, let them run free, innovate, try new things, and minister in creative ways.

50 QUESTION: How does your JH ministry "feel?" The answer may be more important than you think!

Is your ministry stiff, stuffy, and school-like? Or is it real, relational, relevant, and relaxed?

Do students feel like they can be themselves when they walk in your doors, or do they feel the need to keep up facades and appearances?

How a ministry "feels" is, in many ways, the most important part. Your students desperately need a place to relax, be real, express their doubts, and be themselves—a place where, upon entry, the burdens of junior high life are removed for 90 minutes or so.

51 WORRY LESS about being a leader and more about being a shepherd.

I've grown a bit weary of all the leadership lingo! For many people, "leadership" is just an excuse to be lazy. "I don't do the nitty-gritty stuff; I like to cast vision." Newsflash: ANYBODY can cast vision. My teenage son is great at casting vision, and his "visions" usually include a future full of money and pretty ladies.

Instead of focusing on leadership, focus on being a pastor. Determine to be the best shepherd possible to your flock. Tend to your flock, feed your flock, and fend off the wolves. Remember, Jesus called himself the good shepherd, not the good leader.

52 YOU ARE A LEADER— act like one!

I said, "Worry less about being a leader," not "Don't worry at all." You ARE a leader, so act like one! A leader is a servant. A leader gives up some rights for the good of the whole. A leader sees in others what they don't see in themselves. A leader recognizes the direction things need to go and gets the ministry or the team there. A leader knows his strengths and weaknesses. A leader develops a healthy team—not of people who exist only to accomplish her goals, but of empowered initiative-takers.

53 JH MINISTRY— the longer you do it, the less you know!

When I was a 25-year-old junior high pastor, I had been doing it for three years and pretty much knew everything there was to know! Now I'm a 45-year-old junior high pastor, and I realize that I still have so much to learn.

Early adolescence is a roller coaster of emotions and experiences. It is almost impossible for junior highers to figure it all out. My experience has taught me that the same is true for those of us who choose to ride the roller coaster with them!

54 SPIRITUALLY IMMATURE leaders need not apply!

Junior highers are asking questions, doubting their faith, struggling with self-identity, beginning to separate from their parents, and wrestling through friendship issues. And that's just on Monday morning! Because of this, they need mature, Christ-like adults to help them navigate the path they are traveling. Here's an idea: For every young, cool, 18-year-old leader serving in your junior high ministry, try to add an older, wiser one.

55 BUILD A TEAM of leaders who actually like JHers.

Everybody in your church loves junior highers. They have to—it's part of being a Christian. But not everybody in your church LIKES junior highers. Fill your team with adults who actually like junior high students, folks who like the fact that these students are insecure, squirrely, obnoxious, and full of energy. Junior highers need to be led, but they need to be LIKED even more.

56 TELL JH MINISTRY STORIES to anybody in your church who will listen.

Why? Because most people in your church have no clue what is happening in the junior high ministry. They don't sit through a junior high Sunday school meeting or pop into the midweek program or spend a day at camp. If they know anything, they know that the junior high department spilled a cooler full of punch on the fellowship hall carpet. How do they know that? Because the church janitor told the story! Make sure the congregation is hearing the good stories, too.

57 QUESTION: Why does your ministry exist? The answer to that question should always determine what your ministry does.

Does your junior high ministry have a mission statement, a purpose statement, a vision statement, or some sort of written description of why you exist, what you hope to accomplish, or why you do the things you do?

Why is this necessary?

So everybody on your team is unified, pulling on the same side of the rope and paddling in the same direction.

PARENT
MINISTRY

58 **MOST PARENTS** of JHers need two things: hope and help. Look for creative ways to provide a little bit of both.

You don't need to be a parent yourself to encourage those who are. And you certainly don't need to be an expert in all things related to raising junior highers. Most of the parents—and stepparents or guardians or grandparents serving in a parental role—in your ministry just need a little hope and a little help. Hope says, "Hang in there; you are doing a great job." Help says, "Here is a book, article, website, or something else that I think you may find beneficial."

59 **WORK WITH PARENTS,** not AGAINST them— make them your ally, not your enemy.

Not too long ago I met a young junior high youth worker who said, "I don't need parents involved with my ministry. They are the ones making most of the mess my ministry has to clean up!" He viewed parents as the enemy, the ones making it difficult to do his job. And sadly, with a mindset like that, they always will be.

60 **EQUIP PARENTS** to disciple their JHers; don't do it all on their behalf.

Most Christian parents want to be the primary disciplers of their children, but they don't know where to start. Perhaps they tried once or twice and struggled. Maybe they don't really know how to help *themselves* grow—let alone their children! This is a GREAT place to employ a little "hope and help" by letting them know they are capable and providing them with a few simple tools to help them get started.

61 **BUT WHAT ABOUT PARENTS** who aren't Christians?

This is why we in the church can't completely abandon our role as disciplers. Because some parents are unwilling or unable to help their children grow in their faith, your junior high ministry needs to include spiritual growth elements in its programs.

62 **THREE KEYS** to ministering to parents: Earn their trust, earn their trust, and earn their trust!

My friend Katie Edwards has a favorite saying: "If parents are for you, who can be against you?" The more that parents feel they trust you and the junior high ministry, the more influence they allow you to have over their child—and the more they will allow you to speak into their own lives, too.

63 **WHAT NOT TO SAY TO A PARENT:** "I know you are disappointed, but she is only copying the behavior modeled at home."

OK, I know you would never say something like that. But the point is, you often will think and sometimes will be tempted to actually say stuff to parents that simply isn't fair. Now that I have raised two junior high children of my own, I'm embarrassed by some of the judgmental and arrogant things I said to myself (and on more than one occasion, to parents) about how to raise kids. When tempted to give too much advice to parents, practice the art of holding your tongue.

64 IF YOU WOULDN'T SAY IT, play it, or show it with parents in the room, then don't say it, play it, or show it!

This simple little rule has kept me in line (and out of hot water) countless times. Anytime I'm tempted to lead a game that feels a little dangerous or say a joke that feels a little edgy, I ask myself if I would mind parents seeing or hearing it for themselves. If I have a hard time answering the question, I know my answer!

65 PULL A PARENT ASIDE and share something positive about their child.

It's easy—and very encouraging! Parents tend to focus on one of two things: the shortcomings of their child or the shortcomings of their parenting skills. When you take a moment to share something positive about a son or daughter, it is like a glass of cool water to somebody dying of thirst! And the reality is that you can think of SOMETHING positive to say about EVERY student in your group. Here are some easy examples:

"Hey Mr. Jones, Brian was so kind to a new student tonight—it really was neat to watch!"

"Hey Mrs. Garcia, I was so proud of Monica tonight. She stacked chairs without being asked!"

"Hey Mr. Goober, I thought you'd like to know that Kyle didn't pick his nose as much as usual tonight!"

66 CONSIDER CREATING a "Been There, Done That" ministry.

A "Been There, Done That" ministry is simply a ministry to parents consisting of other parents who have expressed willingness to walk their peers through struggles of raising junior highers, struggles they have already been through— and lived to tell the tale!

- A single mom willing to have coffee with a mom who suddenly finds herself raising a junior higher all alone.

- A dad who struggled because his son wasn't interested in sports willing to share his story with another dad in the same boat.

- A couple with a highly rebellious daughter willing to share their insights with another couple going through the same tough season.

67 HAVE AN "OPEN-DOOR" POLICY
that encourages parents to pop in unannounced.

I want the parents in our ministry to know they can visit our weekly gathering to check things out at any time. An open-door policy accomplishes two things:

1. Builds instant trust. You must not be doing stupid stuff if parents are allowed to drop in unannounced.

2. Increases awareness. Many parents have absolutely no idea what is happening in your ministry. An open-door policy allows them to take a quick look, and 99 times out of 100, they like what they see.

68 LET PARENTS know what's happening...

Here's a newsflash: Parents like to know what's coming up and how much it's going to cost. They like to know what you're teaching. They like to know the deadline for camp registration. Emails, texts, printed calendars, a website that is actually updated, Facebook, a Twitter account—there are so many easy ways to keep parents in the loop, there's no excuse not to do it. Pick one or two communication strategies, and consistently utilize them!

69 ...BUT EMBRACE the fact that they still won't know!

If I had a nickel for every time I've heard a parent say, "I had no idea about _____," I would have approximately 932 nickels. Just because I handed a camp form to a kid doesn't mean the kid handed it to mom. Just because we have a Facebook page doesn't mean dads are checking it out for details about the father/son trip. Use these moments as opportunities to remind parents of the communication methods you employ, and encourage them to take advantage of those methods.

70 WHEN PLANNING ACTIVITIES, REMEMBER: Parents have to be willing to drive their kids there.

Because parents are the mode of transportation for junior highers, plan your activities and events with this in mind. Have events begin and end at times that are convenient for parents. Most parents don't like to get out of bed at (or stay awake until) 2 a.m., so that may not be the most strategic time to have your activity end.

71 WHEN IT COMES TO INFLUENCE in a JHer's life, youth workers should be the vitamins; parents are the meal.

As a caring adult, your role is to supplement the influence of mom and dad. You should never try to replace the influence of parents, but sometimes your influence will make up for insufficiencies at home. Parents, relatives, youth workers, coaches, teachers, and other caring adults all combine for a well-balanced "influence diet" for junior highers, but it's important to remember that the largest chunk of influence, for good and for bad, comes from home.

RANDOM
STUFF

72 **KEEP A PICTURE HANDY** from your JH days; remembering what it was like for you will help you consider what it's like for them!

On the desktop of my laptop, I have my eighth-grade picture. I look at it quite often. Partly because I like to remember what I looked like with more hair and fewer "smile wrinkles," but also because it helps me remember what it is like to be in junior high.

73 **THE LITTLE THINGS** often make the biggest difference.

Remembering students' names upon their second visit to the group, following up on a prayer request, sending a handwritten birthday card in the mail. It is often the things that are seemingly small and "routine" that make the longest-lasting impact. Become a master of the little things!

74 **STICK AROUND.**

Good things happen all the time, but GREAT things usually take a little longer. Here are just a few of the great things that longevity breeds:

- Former students wander back into the junior high room to share what God is doing in their lives, and you are still there to hear about it!

- Former students are now old enough to serve in the junior high ministry, and you are still there to serve alongside and mentor them.

- The junior high ministry gains credibility in the church because adult leaders like yourself have deemed it worthy of your investment.

- The quality and impact of the junior high ministry increases because it is being led by skilled veterans.

75 LEARN FROM THE JH MINISTRY down the street, across town, and across the country.

It's arrogant to think the church down the street has nothing to offer you just because it's bigger, smaller, of another denomination, or has a different theological bent. A wise man once said, "There is nothing new under the sun," which means there's probably no awesome junior high idea that pops into your mind that hasn't already popped into somebody else's mind—and been put into action! Don't let your pride get in the way of your willingness to share your expertise and borrow the expertise of others.

76 "COOL" IS OVERRATED.

Don't let yourself buy into the hype. You don't have to have a cool tattoo to be an effective junior high youth worker. Your junior high room doesn't need cool lights, and your lessons don't have to be filled with cool gimmicks. Cool is overrated, and flash rarely lasts.

77 PARTNER WITH YOUR CHILDREN'S MINISTRY. I repeat, partner with your children's ministry!

Ask leaders from the children's ministry questions about the incoming junior highers, create a teaching strategy that builds upon what students were taught in the children's ministry, partner with them to minister to families and parents, and pursue other cooperative strategies. Avoid the temptation to belittle your children's ministry with jokes about sock puppets, flannel boards, and animal crackers. As funny as that stuff may be (and it is really funny), it doesn't serve to create unity.

78 MAKE YOURSELF AVAILABLE to public school teachers and administrators.

Make it a goal to meet every junior high principal in your area. Let the school counselors know who you are, and let local school officials know that you would love to partner with them in any way they would like. I'm always confused when youth workers choose to take an adversarial approach to the public school system. Instead, look for ways to bless schools, teachers, and administrators at every turn.

79 BECOME A MASTER at asking open-ended questions.

Junior highers are experts at giving one-word—or one-grunt—answers, so eliminate the option!

Instead of merely asking if they had a good day, ask them to tell you a little bit about their day.

During Bible study, avoid asking, "According to this verse, does God want us to honor our parents?" Frame the question differently by saying something like, "This verse makes it clear God wants us to honor our parents—but why is that sometimes such a hard thing to do?"

By asking open-ended questions, you help set the stage for deeper, longer, more meaningful conversations. There will still be an occasional grunt—but it least it will be surrounded by a few words!

80 **PRACTICE THE ART** of the second chance.

Few people will try your patience like junior highers; give them a second chance.

Few people will mess up as often as junior highers; give them a second chance.

Few people are as likely as a junior higher to pass gas in the middle of your lesson; give them a second chance. (Then they'll pass gas a second time!)

One of the best ways to help your junior highers understand the power of God's grace is to model it to them yourself.

81 **THE SECOND VISIT IS MORE IMPORTANT THAN THE FIRST,** so treat second-time guests well.

A return visit means they liked what they saw. They felt comfortable enough to give things a second try. Lots of kids visit church once, never to be seen again. But the ones who are seen again have the potential to stick around! Think of creative ways to give extra attention to second-time visitors because getting second-timers to become regular attenders is a great way to grow your ministry.

82 GO WHERE JHERS ARE; don't always expect them to come to you.

If the only time you interact with junior highers is when they come to church, you are missing a wonderful world of ministry opportunity! Go to the local movie theater on a Friday night. Volunteer as a lunch aide once a month. Be a Little League® umpire. Do whatever it takes to find ways to see and be seen by junior highers outside the confines of your church.

83 WATCH WHAT THEY WATCH , read what they read, and listen to what they listen to—at least sometimes!

Buy a skateboarding magazine, watch an occasional episode of the TV show your seventh-grade girls can't stop talking about, download a song or two from the band that is the current flavor of the month.

You don't need to know everything about the stuff your junior highers are into, but you don't want to know *nothing* about it, either.

84 YOUR JH MINISTRY is like a slice of pizza.

I stole this idea from my buddy Mark Oestreicher. (Remember my thought about learning from others?) Here's the idea: Think of your ministry as a slice of pizza, with each student being a unique topping. Somebody is the pepperoni, somebody else the cheese. Somebody is the olive, and somebody else the anchovy! All junior highers are needed because they add flavor and texture to the pizza! Without their presence, your "pizza" would be missing something wonderful.

85 BUY A FEW *Uncle John's Bathroom Reader* books.

These things have been around forever, and they are still cranking out new ones! These books are a terrific source of odd trivia, interesting facts, and quirky cultural insights. You can purchase individual books or the big multivolume editions. The more you dig around these bad boys, the more uses you will find. For samples visit bathroomreader.com.

86 MEMORIZE a few easy games to play when you need to kill some time because the church van broke down (again).

One key to junior high ministry success is spontaneity. And the ability to play a spontaneous game or two will serve you well. Here is a freebie:

Game: "The Look Up Game" (creative title, I know)

Object: Be the last player (or players) standing.

How to Play: Players stand in a circle, looking down with their eyes closed. On the count of three, everybody quickly looks up and immediately stares at another player. If you happen to be staring at a player who is also staring at you, you are both out. If you are staring at someone who is staring at someone else, you get to keep playing. Repeat until only one or two players remain.

87 IF SOMETHING GOES WRONG, tell your supervisor about it right away.

If (when) something goes wrong, about the only way to make it worse is for your supervisor to hear about it from someone else. I'm pretty sure your supervisor wants to have your back, but it is tough when they get surprised with bad news. When bad things happen, swallow hard and give your supervisor a call. (In politics, this would be called "getting out in front of the story.") Your supervisor doesn't want to know about the fact that Johnny forgot it was his night to bring snacks or that your lesson went three minutes long, but that person does want to know, from you, that you miscounted and left a student at camp.

88 PERSONAL, HANDWRITTEN notes never go out of style.

In fact, in this age of social media and texting, a handwritten note might be something your junior highers have never received! The old can suddenly become new! Introduce your students to the thrill of receiving a letter or postcard in the mail. Their parents may have to explain what that strange, sealed envelope thingy is, but your students will catch on—and they'll like it.

89 IF YOU WANT TO KEEP RESTAURANTS, hotels, and the church janitor happy, leave it better than you found it!

Junior highers have a terrible reputation of being slobs. And rightly so. Servers tremble in fear when they see a group of junior highers enter their eating establishment. Hotel managers develop eye twitches after a group of young teenagers stays overnight. Many a church janitor has lost his salvation due to the cuss words messy junior highers have caused him to utter. Maybe your group can be different.

90 REMEMBERING a name is the first step into a heart.

It has been said that a student's name is their most precious possession. I agree, and I would add that it is actually much more than a "possession"—it is a massive part of their identity. That's why your ability to remember it is a big deal. I'm the king of calling guys "dude" and addressing girls as "hey, girl!" I've seen eyes light up when I remember a name I shouldn't, and I've seen them fade when I forget a name I should know. I'll make you a deal: I'll get better at remembering names if you do, too.

91 DO YOURSELF A FAVOR; never again ask, "What were you thinking?"

Students won't give you the answer you want to hear, and if they gave you the honest answer, you wouldn't want to hear it! Because the honest answer is, THEY WEREN'T THINKING! Most of the time, junior highers do first and sometimes think later.

92 EMBARRASS YOURSELF. You'll be forever famous.

Once a year, I tell the story about a bird pooping on my shoulder right as the bell rang on the first day of school. It is a classic.

A few years ago, I went head over heels as I was trying to run off the stage while pushing a wheelbarrow. The story is legendary in my parts.

Don't play the goof or the class clown; that gets old in a hurry. But when goofy, embarrassing things happen, capitalize on those moments.

93 LISTEN MORE THAN YOU SPEAK.

You may have lots of great things to say, but you don't always need to say them. Instead, develop the skill of listening more than you speak. Listening to your students helps you learn, and the more you learn, the richer your words become. Immature leaders feel the need to always give an answer, a word of advice, or an exhortation. The time to speak will come, but probably not as quickly as you think it should.

94 JH MINISTRY is like mixing concrete.

For years we took our junior highers on a mission trip to Mexico to build homes for impoverished families. The toughest part of the job was hand-mixing the concrete. We would spend an entire day mixing concrete to form an 11-foot-by-22-foot foundation. It was BRUTAL work, but we knew that if we didn't mix the concrete and build a good foundation, we wouldn't be able to build the rest of the house.

Junior high ministry is the concrete-mixing part of youth ministry. It is hard, backbreaking work, but you are helping to build a foundation upon which so much else will be built!

95 **BULLYING SUCKS;** don't tolerate it.

Bullying, hazing, mean-spirited teasing—you know it when you see it. And when you see it, put a stop to it! Dead legs, using rolled-up towels to create a "rat tail," pink bellies, swirlies, and the like may sound like fun but almost always escalate and can have far-reaching ramifications.

96 **STUDENTS' HEARTS ARE SOFT,** so wisely expose them to the needs of those who are less fortunate.

The world is hurting, and there is much to be done to help the oppressed, poor, and neglected. Look for age-appropriate opportunities to expose your students to the plight of the less fortunate, but avoid the temptation to use shock, guilt, and hyperbole. And remember, there is such a thing as too much, too soon.

97 **LET STUDENTS SEE YOUR FLAWS AND QUIRKS;** it will help them be comfortable with their own.

Junior highers need to be around adults who are real and aren't afraid to show their "realness." You are a flawed, quirky human being who is loved and accepted by God. If you can model being comfortable in your own skin, you will help junior highers feel more comfortable in theirs.

98 IF YOU ARE HAVING FUN, invite somebody to join you.

The world needs more adults who are willing to invest in the lives of young teenagers. If you are enjoying it, don't keep junior high ministry a secret! You know what it takes to be an effective junior high youth worker, and chances are you have a friend or two who might fit the bill. I've learned over the years that the best way to recruit new volunteers is through current volunteers. That's right, YOU are the best recruitment strategy your church has.

99 FINALLY, KNOW THAT YOU ARE MAKING A DIFFERENCE!

It may not always feel like it, and the behavior in the seventh-grade boys Sunday school class will try to convince you otherwise, but what you are doing matters—it matters a lot. And the time you are investing today will pay off for all eternity. You are making a difference, and if you haven't heard it in a while, let me say it loud and clear: THANK YOU!